Original title:
The Joy of Not Knowing

Copyright © 2025 Creative Arts Management OÜ
All rights reserved.

Author: Mariana Leclair
ISBN HARDBACK: 978-1-80566-180-1
ISBN PAPERBACK: 978-1-80566-475-8

Treasures of the Unanswered

In a world of guessing games,
We trip on all life's silly names.
Questions bloom like wildflowers,
Under clouds of fleeting hours.

Maps of mystery we draw,
With breadcrumbs of the strange and raw.
What's the secret in that hat?
Maybe it's a sleeping cat!

A Serenade for the Curious

Oh, the things we ponder late,
Like why do ducks migrate in straight?
Silly thoughts a-buzz and whirl,
Like twirls of a dizzying pearl.

What's a cloud's favorite snack?
Maybe it's a fluffy black pack!
We strum the strings of our amazed,
With laughter in the dizzy glaze.

Petals of Possibility

Each petal holds a whisper sweet,
Of mysteries beneath our feet.
What if birds decide to dance?
Grabbing worms with a sideways glance!

The trees debate on when to leaf,
With branches shaking in belief.
Oh, the giggles in the breeze,
Chasing shadows with such ease.

The Euphoria of Odysseys

Wandering paths where no one's been,
Chasing laughter, catching the tin.
Is that a unicorn or just a dog?
Both seem legit in this fog!

With maps that twist and turn like fate,
We laugh at roads that wait and wait.
Unraveled yarns and tangled tales,
All aboard for silly gales!

The Allure of Mystery

In shadows where secrets play,
Curiosity leads the way.
With doubt as my quirky friend,
Every twist feels like a trend.

Why does the toaster pop its toast?
Is it a ghost that likes to boast?
Each oddity sparks my delight,
Unsolved puzzles take to flight.

Beyond the Horizon of Certainty

Who needs a map for this grand ride?
I trust my instincts, not the guide.
Wandering off the beaten track,
I never fear a single lack.

Will I find treasure or just a shoe?
It's hard to tell, but I'll get through.
With every step, my heart does dance,
Embracing fate's whimsical chance.

Thrill of the Unexplored

An unopened box, what could it hold?
A knitted sweater or tales of old?
With no blueprints drawn to confine,
Adventure waits for a silly sign.

The mystery fruit in the fridge stares,
What color is it? Who really cares?
With a fork and a wink, I'll dive right in,
Life's curious treats are a delicious sin.

Infinite Possibilities Await

A world of options, all askew,
Should I be dressed as a pirate or boo?
With a grin I'll twirl, and round I'll go,
Into the wild unknowns that flow.

Cereal for dinner? Why not both?
Life's little quirks induce some growth.
At the crossroads of wrong and right,
I'll dance between laugh and silly fright.

Euphoria of Every Question

Why do cats dance in the rain?

They know something we don't explain.

Tarzan swings through forests of doubt,

While squirrels plot foot races about.

Is the moon really made of cheese?

Or is it just there to tease?

Every riddle's a trick or a treat,

Like ice cream soup—oh so neat!

When will I learn the secret code?

Maybe it starts with a silly ode.

Lost cats sing lullabies at night,

As giggles float past, out of sight.

The Allure of What Lies Ahead

Last week I baked a cake by chance,

It turned into a pancake dance.

What's behind door number three?

A llama dressed as a jubilee!

If I ask where socks disappear,

Will I get answers or just a sneer?

Balloons lead a parade on their own,

While jellybeans party, they're never alone.

Sailing ships on rivers of fog,

Join hands with the moonlit dog.

Will I ever chase kittens in my dreams?

Or settle down with Netflix and memes?

A Canvas of Ambiguous Hues

What paint will my spaghetti choose?

To brighten this canvas and amuse?

Shall I mix purple with some bright green?

Or splash blue around like I'm never seen?

Mysteries drip like ice cream cones,

Wonders jump like old-fashioned phones.

Rainbows hide behind curious feet,

As jellybeans throw a wild beat.

A shoe for the moon, a hat for the sun,

Mismatched outfits for every fun run.

Who says colors must fit in a line?

Life is better when it twirls and twines!

Serenity in the Unpredictable

What flavor is the fluttering breeze?

Is it minty fresh, or just leaves?

Do ants sketch plans in the dirt?

Or is the universe just a weird flirt?

Today I wore shoes made of cheese,

And danced with crickets under the trees.

Will I ride a wave on a jellyfish?

Or float on clouds that grant any wish?

A shoe parade with no end in sight,

As hot dogs debate the meaning of light.

In this chaos, I find that I cheer,

For strange is just splendid when it's sincere.

Sipping from the Well of Surprise

I took a sip from a cup of air,
A taste of giggles, beyond compare.
What's in the puddle? I dare not ask,
Just splash around, it's a charming task.

With every gulp, my mind takes flight,
Dancing with bubbles in the moonlight.
Oh look, a fish that wears a tie!
I wonder how it learned to fly?

Emptiness and Ecstasy

In a jar of nothing, I found some bliss,
An empty promise sealed with a kiss.
My cat wore a hat, thought he was grand,
The emptiness danced, took my hand.

In the silence, I hear a scream,
A melody lost in a wild dream.
What's hiding there? I know not yet,
But I'll jest and twirl with no regret.

Finding Magic in the Unexplained

A cloud shapes a whale, or is it a shoe?
I laugh at the sky, what else is new?
The trees tell stories, a chuckle or two,
Why not believe in a dragon or two?

Where do socks go, the lost and the free?
They play hide and seek, just wait and see!
Caught in a loop of silly delight,
Each moment a treasure, shining bright.

Unfurling the Map of Imagination

I found a map that leads nowhere,
With dotted lines and a cupcake bear.
Each tick of the clock, a noodle of fun,
Why search for answers when we can run?

A pirate's hat made of whipped cream,
Sailing through clouds on a gummy dream.
Who needs a compass, my dog has a plan,
To chase the shadows and tease the sand.

Trails of Uncertainty

I wandered with no map in hand,
Lost in a land so vast and grand.
I met a squirrel asking for cheese,
While trying to catch a sneeze.

A path that twisted like a vine,
Led me to a sign that said 'Divine!'
But all it meant was a pie shop near,
With blueberry filling - oh dear, oh dear!

My shoes got muddy, what a delight,
Every twist and turn a funny sight.
I laughed with clouds that drifted by,
And danced with shadows, oh me, oh my!

What treasures lie without a clue?
I found a hat that looked like a shoe.
The less I knew, the more I played,
In this wacky world, my troubles decayed.

Colors of the Unanswered

A canvas blank, no paint to use,
Dipped my brush in shades of blues.
I splashed yellow, maybe red,
Created a monster with three heads!

Each stroke brought giggles, what a blend,
Of colors mixed that'd never end.
No answer sought, no rules to reign,
Just funny shapes that danced in rain.

An elephant waltzed on a green polka dot,
Alongside a cat that could juggle a pot.
With every smudge, my joy took flight,
In a world of nonsense, oh what a sight!

The laughter rang from each mishap,
As splatters formed a silly map.
Who knows the answer to my wild art?
It's just pure fun that fills the heart!

Embracing the Uncharted

I took a step, no plan in mind,
To sail the seas where waves unwind.
The compass spun in circles wide,
As I splashed in the ocean's tide.

A pirate parrot squawked at me,
"Why not try the chocolate tea?"
I grabbed a mug and sipped with glee,
And discovered it was actually brie!

The ship went left, then turned around,
A chase with dolphins under the sound.
"Do you know where we're heading next?"
They laughed and said, "We're so perplexed!"

Each wave a giggle, each gust a cheer,
We sailed on joy, with no fear near.
For maps can wait, let whims take flight,
In the uncharted, everything's bright!

Whispers of Uncertainty

I heard a rumor down the lane,
That marshmallows fall like rain.
With open mouth, I stood amazed,
As chocolate chips in sunbeams blazed.

The sky was grey, or perhaps it gleamed,
And every taste was what I dreamed.
A lollipop tree danced in the breeze,
Whispering secrets to buzzing bees.

The neighbors chuckled, "What a scene!
With gummy bears in place of beans!"
I joined the fun, no reason to fret,
In this odd world, I placed my bet.

Who needs the facts when fun's the game?
In whispers sweet, all's never the same.
Let laughter lead wherever I go,
In the sweet unknown, I find my flow!

Dreams in the Fog

Waking up, what day is it?
Did I really wear this tie?
My coffee's cold, my socks don't match,
Yet somehow, I still fly.

Clouds are drifting, quite the scene,
A cat just taught me how to dance.
I chase my thoughts that run away,
In this whimsical riddle, there's chance.

Laughter echoes down the street,
A man in flip-flops, how absurd!
He waves at birds, they seem to greet,
Lost in a world without a word.

Oh surprise, the cake's upside down,
Each slice a puzzle to unseal.
Frosting roads in a doughnut town,
These little quirks are quite the deal.

The Symphony of Unfathomed Paths

Musical notes in the air swirl,
A rogue squirrel sings a tune,
I try to dance, my shoes betray,
A comedy of feet in June.

Paths untaken twist and twirl,
Maps just laugh and call me 'fool'.
I step in puddles, rainbows gleam,
Where am I going? Who needs a rule?

Frogs in tuxedos leap in style,
They croak their wisdom, dressed to please.
Maybe life's just one big smile,
With lazy thoughts hanging from trees.

Lemonade rivers flow with zest,
I follow the laughter, not the plan.
Each wrong turn is a bubbling jest,
Oh look—there goes another fan!

Radiance in Riddles

On a sunny day, I wear a hat,
Made from yesterday's 'what-ifs'.
I stroll through dreams, full of splats,
Life is sweeter with some myths.

Mysteries laced in spaghetti strands,
Twirling thoughts dance in my mind.
I trip on jokes, fall not on plans,
In this carnival of the blind.

Juggling worries like oranges bright,
A clown pops up—then bids adieu.
Balloons parade into the night,
I wonder what he wished to do.

Puzzles wrapped in a bright gift box,
I shake and guess—oh what a thrill.
Maybe it's shoes or laughing socks,
Surprises come without a drill!

Captivated by the Infinite

A door swings open, wait, what's this?
A wardrobe hides an espresso bar.
I sip and dream of endless bliss,
While chasing after a falling star.

Footprints wander without a care,
Guide me, please to where I'm bound.
Is it wrong to lose the air?
In this chaos, joy is found.

Time skips like stones on a pond,
Every ripple a riddle to crack.
I play hide-and-seek with a blond,
She giggles softly, never looks back.

Rain dances down in a silly spree,
As umbrellas fly like frisbees grand.
In the unknown, I am free,
What's around the bend? Just take my hand!

Serendipity in Unfamiliarity

Stumbled upon a road so strange,
Where signs were mixed, and squirrels exchanged.
A fountain flowed with soda pop,
I guess today, we just won't stop!

Maps are outdated, who needs a guide?
We'll sail on confetti, take joy in the ride.
With every twist, a new laugh to find,
In this wacky world, let's unwind our mind!

Cacti wear hats, and trees sing tunes,
A dance-off with ducks under glowing moons.
We welcomed each blunder with a happy cheer,
In the land of the quirky, there's nothing to fear!

So toss away caution, let's wander and roam,
For every wrong turn feels just like home.
Adventure awaits in the strangest of places,
With giggles and grins on all of our faces.

Laughter in the Void

I jumped into a puddle, oh what a splash,
Turns out it's gelatin, a quivering clash!
Beware of the clouds, they're watching too close,
One wink and a gust could turn you to toast!

A lion played cards with a jellybean witch,
They tugged at their beards, looking for a snitch.
A balloon on the lam, oh what a scene,
He floated away with a hope and a dream!

Earthquakes of laughter erupted upside down,
Pigeons in tuxedos strutted in town.
In the void, there's chaos, a carnival bright,
As we giggle at shadows in the flickering light!

So let's embrace the unknown with a wink and a twist,
For every madcap moment we shall not miss!
Joy rides on laughter, a kite in the air,
In the void, we discover how much we can share.

Curiosity's Delight

I wobbled on stilts made of pasta and cheese,
While juggling with pickles that danced in the breeze.
With quirky inventions found under my bed,
Like a toaster that sings when it's buttering bread!

Oh, the things we might taste if we dare to explore,
A cupcake that giggles or a muffin that soars.
Curiosity sparks like a cake made of foam,
With each silly trip, we find ourselves home.

Invisible cats play hopscotch with glee,
They chase after rainbows, just wait and you'll see!
In wonderment's playground, where oddities roam,
Every question we ask leads to frolicsome loam!

So let's tiptoe through whimsies, take chances galore,
With laughter as our compass, we'll never be bored.
In this curious dance, let's leap and unite,
Find treasures in questions, ignite our delight!

Floating in Possibility

Caught on a feather, I floated away,
To a land full of gumdrops and tea brewed from clay.
Where dreams wear pajamas and twirl in the sun,
Every hour is happy, let folly be fun!

I asked a wise turtle for secrets galore,
He responded with giggles and opened a door.
In a world of balloons filled with laughter and cheer,
The only wrong answer is to live out of fear!

A cake once told me that wishes come true,
If given some sprinkles and chocolate to chew.
With friends made of marshmallows, we skate on the breeze,
In the land where the silly plays tag with the trees!

So drift through the clouds, let your dreams take a ride,
In the canvas of chance, let your spirit decide.
For floating in possibility offers delight,
And every new whim is a reason to write!

Colors of a Blank Page

A canvas waits with open arms,
Where brushes dance without alarms.
A splash of pink, a dot of green,
What's next, oh what could it mean?

With eyes closed tight, we throw a swirl,
A mysterious hue in a twirling whirl.
Is that a cow or maybe a shoe?
It's art, my friend! Not meant to be true!

We giggle as we mix up shades,
Who knew blue could come in cascades?
Let's paint a frog that sings in tune,
Underneath a purple moon!

So here's to colors wild and free,
On this blank page, just wait and see.
We'll scribble here with joyful grace,
And laugh at our own painted face!

Finding Magic in Vagueness

In the fog, where ideas hide,
A twisty path, a fun-filled ride.
What's that sound? A swoosh, a bump,
Oh, just a squirrel with a little jump!

Let's toss confetti made of fluff,
In this blurry world, we can feel tough.
A mop could be a dancing broom,
Shaking in our gloomy room!

Surprises lurk in every glance,
Embrace the mist, it's like a dance.
Is that a cat or just a shadow?
Maybe both, but who can know?

A riddle found in half a word,
A gummy bear that just prefers,
To float around without a care,
In this vague realm, we'll always dare!

Revelry in Improv

Step right up, it's showtime dear!
We'll make it up, bring on the cheer!
A llama in a tutu prances by,
With juggling pies, oh my, oh my!

What's the scene? A beach or a cave?
Nonsense is the ride, so let's be brave!
I'm a sandwich, you're a chair,
In this wild play, we're everywhere!

The plot may twist, the lines may bend,
Each silly moment, we won't offend.
Who needs a script when laughs abound?
In our make-believe, silliness is found!

Join the parade of crazy thought,
With every step, a giggle's caught.
Improv life is the best charade,
Where we craft joy in masquerade!

Chasing the Undiscovered

Oh, what's that hiding in the grass?
A treasure map or just a mass?
I'll track the winds and chase the new,
With my trusty sidekick, a rubber shoe!

A mystery box? Open it wide!
A bunch of socks or a dinosaur's ride?
Let's search for gold or silly quotes,
In our grand quest with mismatched coats!

An unknown path leads us away,
Through giggles, jumps, and a bit of play.
What lies ahead? Only a guess,
But who needs plans when fun's the best?

So here we go, hold on tight!
Adventure calls, it's pure delight.
We'll laugh and dance, what more can we wish?
In the realm of the unknown, we'll find our dish!

Marvels of the Undefined

In a world where questions dance,
And answers play a game of chance,
I wear my hat of curious glee,
For nothing's quite as fun as free.

The map is blank, the path unclear,
Yet joy bubbles up, it's quite sincere,
Like socks that vanish without a trace,
Embracing life's whimsical, funny race.

Every corner hides a brand new tale,
Like finding treasure on a movie trail,
The silly moments, unmatched delight,
In the undefined, we take flight.

So cheers to fumbles, stumbles too,
With secret codes none of us knew,
Let's toast to the chaos, wild and bright,
For it's the unknown that feels just right!

Unveiling Secrets of the Future

What will tomorrow bring, I ask,
A flying pig, or a sunny flask?
The crystal ball just winks and sighs,
While laughter bubbles up, oh my!

Mysteries hide in cupboards and drawers,
A life of giggles, behind closed doors,
Every 'who knows' is a treasure chest,
With silly wonders, we feel so blessed.

The future dances, a jester's jig,
Like chasing shadows that laugh and dig,
We spin in circles, our hearts aglow,
In every moment, the thrill of the show.

So let's embrace what's out of sight,
With goofy hopes, our spirits bright,
For certainty is simply a bore,
In the future's riddle, who needs more?

The Gift of Uncertainty

Oh, the gifts of life, wrapped in surprise,
Like missing keys and strange alibis,
Every plan that took a detour ride,
Turns into laughter, we can't abide.

Will today be chaos, or maybe bliss?
I'll take the wild, I'll take the miss,
A twist of fate, a dance so rare,
Life's a comedy, with giggles to share.

In the unplanned moments, we find a spark,
Like tripping over a cat in the dark,
A riddle of sorts that leaves us in stitches,
Dancing on life's unpredictable pitches.

So let's unwrap life's finest jokes,
With each surprise, our spirit pokes,
The gift of not knowing, pure and bright,
A sprinkle of laughter in every night!

Chasing Mystery's Embrace

In the woods of doubt, I chase a sound,
What's that rustling, the tales abound?
Like chasing shadows that seem to prance,
Life's a riddle, let's take a chance!

Every question is a quirky clue,
A mischievous sprite whispering too,
I leap through puzzles with carefree glee,
In the absurd, we find the key.

What's behind door number unknown?
A dancing llama, or a talking stone?
With open hearts, let's explore the maze,
Where laughter echoes and surprises blaze.

So here's to the chase, to the chase of fun,
In the quirkiest moments, we've already won,
For life's a comic play, we laugh and embrace,
Chasing mystery with a silly grace!

Savoring the Unseen

In the fridge, I found a jar,
What's inside? A mystery afar.
Is it pickles or jam gone wrong?
I'll just pop it open and sing a song.

The sky hides clouds like a sneaky cat,
Will it rain? I do not know that.
I'll twirl in puddles, take my chance,
For every drop could lead to a dance.

The game of life is quite absurd,
With questions flying like a startled bird.
I raised my hand, but forgot my name,
And then I tripped—oops, what a game!

Maps are drawn in invisible ink,
Where am I going? I just can't think.
But winding paths are more than fun,
Let's see where the next adventure runs.

The Freedom in Questioning

What's that noise? A ghost or a cat?
I'll poke my head, the thrill is where it's at.
Maybe it's pizza calling my name,
Or just the fridge playing a silly game.

Should I wear socks or mismatched shoes?
Either would do, I cannot lose.
Life's a circus of curious sights,
I'll juggle my doubts and leap in fright.

Is it too late for cake or cheer?
The clock is ticking, but who's keeping near?
With every bite, a grin does sprout,
Guilty pleasures chased without a doubt.

Chasing shadows in the bright sunlight,
Are they monsters or merely delight?
With laughter echoing through the air,
I'll follow whims without a care.

A Tapestry of Surprises

Crayon drawings on a napkin bright,
What do they mean? Oh, what a sight!
Perhaps a dragon, or a fish named Fred,
Who needs logic when you can paint instead?

In a box labeled 'Do Not Open',
A world awaits, unspoken and woven.
Could it be treasures, or just old socks?
I'll take my chances, let's not be foxed!

With every twist, the story unfolds,
A sock puppet whispers secrets untold.
My pet goldfish might be a wise sage,
Who needs a script on this crazy stage?

As I dance through life's playful maze,
Surprises pop up in so many ways.
What's next, who knows? It's a delightful craze,
In this carnival of maybes, let's set ablaze!

Sudden Twists and Turns

On the road, I took a left out of blue,
Why'd I do that? Unclear, it's true.
But there's excitement in the unexpected,
With each laughable bump, I feel connected.

Found a plot twist in my cereal bowl,
What's that? A marshmallow giant, oh, so whole!
I'll build a fortress, make it my throne,
Why worry about breakfast when joy is grown?

Adventure awaits in the strangest places,
Like tripping down stairs while making faces.
My rubber chicken clucks quite a song,
With twists that keep me rolling along.

Here's to chaos and navigating fate,
With a wink and a giggle, let's celebrate.
Life's clumsy dance is filled with glee,
In this goofy world, I'll always be free!

Whispers of the Unseen

In the land of 'Who Knows?' I roam,
With socks mismatched, I feel at home.
The secrets hide behind the door,
I laugh and trip, then search for more.

A squirrel debates, should it be fat?
Am I lost? Maybe. Should I chat?
Lost my keys and found a shoe,
At least the squirrels got a clue!

Maps are for sailors; I'm a guy,
Who wheels around on a donut pie.
The clocks are broken, and so am I,
But the sunshine's high, oh me, oh my!

So here I dance, all spry and funny,
With pockets full of dreams and honey.
The road's unclear, but hey, that's fine,
Let's toast to life with grape soda wine!

The Beauty of Uncharted Paths

A compass spins like a wild top,
Each step I take feels like a flop.
But every flop's a chance to play,
I greet the clouds, "What's up today?"

The trees are puzzled: "Where's he going?"
I answer, "I don't know, but keep it glowing!"
Behind the bushes, a rabbit sings,
About life and all its silly things.

Serendipitous bumps make me pause,
A little dance for no good cause.
What's this? A puddle? A tiny moat?
Let's jump right in, it looks like a boat!

Wanderlust in mismatched shoes,
A parade of breadcrumbs, what's to lose?
Each twist and turn a laugh, for sure,
Uncharted paths feel like a tour!

Freedom in Not Knowing

Oh, the beauty of a mind adrift,
I flip a coin, it's quite the gift.
Should I jump in? Perhaps I'll slide,
With candy floss strapped to my side!

The cookie jar's empty, who needs a plan?
In jammies, I'm a disco man.
With twirls and spins in a messy kitchen,
I'll bake a cake, or just keep twitchin'.

I rode a bike with the tires flat,
Found my old teddy, gave him a chat.
To each question I throw a shrug,
"Who's driving this boat? Now that's a bug!"

So here I go, on my wandering spree,
With each wrong turn, a new decree.
Forty-two reasons to skip and prance,
Freedom's a laugh, come join the dance!

Reveling in Ambiguity

In a blurry world, I put on a hat,
Not sure if it's a toupee or what's that?
Each corner turned, a circus awaits,
With elephants dressed as farm-shaped mates.

I once woke up beneath a cat,
Questioning how I ended up that.
The clock jumped forward, or was it back?
I'll eat my toast, while making up slack.

With tea leaves reading and a spoon of jam,
I pondered fiercely: "Who's Uncle Sam?"
Oh life, you joker, keep up the ruse,
In mystery's dance, I cannot lose!

So gather 'round, it's all quite absurd,
Laughing at life—an unspoken word.
With every step into the misty nook,
We pen our own tales in this funny book!

Notes from the Unknown

I woke up to the sound of socks,
Missing one, they're playing the box.
What's hiding in the cereal bowl?
A surprise! It's a jelly roll.

The cat is plotting, I can tell,
Dancing around like a tiny rebel.
Is that a ghost or just my toast?
I'm hoping it's the ghost I'd like the most.

A knock, a shuffle, who could it be?
It's the postman with a mystery.
Bills and packages wrapped in cheer,
They all come with a sprinkle of fear.

What's waiting at the end of the road?
A hidden treasure or a heavy load?
I'll bring my shovel just in case,
Turns out it's my shoes; what a funny chase!

Laughter in the Shadows

I heard a joke whispered by the moon,
She said, 'What's that noise? A disco tune?'
The lamp just chuckled, the fridge took a sip,
In this wild party, I'm ready to trip.

A shadow danced, curiously near,
Whispered secrets brought me to cheer.
I surveyed the room full of squeaky chairs,
What's laughing at me? Just my own cares.

The clock chimed softly, I leapt in surprise,
Why is it winking with two playful eyes?
Tomorrow's mystery wrapped tight in a bow,
But tonight, it's just fun in the shadow's glow.

Suddenly, the curtain flew wide with a grin,
'What's in the box? Oh, let's begin!'
A rubber chicken? A hat? A sock?
Or is it just laughter, a playful knock?

Fleeting Moments of Wonder

Here comes a cloud wearing sunglasses,
Is it a bird or just a lot of pizzazzes?
Each raindrop giggles, tumbling down,
In the puddle, a reflection wears a frown.

Butterflies blushing, caught in the breeze,
Do they know why they flutter with ease?
A quick glimpse of daisies, topsy-turvy,
Oh look! A snail, feeling quite swervy.

Lemonade stands that sell bits of cheer,
But today, they've swapped the drinks for a deer!
'What's in that cup?' a passerby said,
He took a sip and watched the shadows spread.

Each glance a giggle, each moment a twist,
How can we plan what we might have missed?
In this fleeting circus of wonder and play,
Every question tickles; every jest is a ray.

Abundance in Ambiguity

The wardrobe's singing, I swear it's true,
It's wearing my shoes, and now it's blue!
What lies behind that quirky door?
A garden of socks, or maybe something more?

The fridge hums softly, adds to the blend,
Is it making dinner or just playing pretend?
A carrot chuckled, bright as a wink,
'There's magic in chaos,' it said with a blink.

Spinning plates with marbles galore,
What's under the table? A duster? A chore?
I poke and I prod, with mischief in eyes,
Each nook hides a secret wrapped in surprise.

In the cupboard, a treasure, oh who knows?
A basket of cakes or a toe with a hose?
Embrace the unknown, let the riddles play,
For in jumbled adventures, we find our way!

In Pursuit of the Unfathomable

Chasing shadows with a grin,
What's around the corner, let's begin!
The mystery dance, a silly chase,
Where all our spoons have lost their place.

We tiptoe through the foggy haze,
Stumbling on in joyous ways.
Why ask questions? Let's pretend,
That the answers just won't bend!

Each twist and turn is full of glee,
Like finding socks that don't agree.
In every wrong, a right await,
With puzzled looks, we meet our fate.

So let's embrace this tangled mess,
With giggles shared and no duress.
The fun's in not knowing what's next,
In this absurdity, we're blessed!

Revelations in the Dark

Whispers in the midnight air,
Looking for lost socks everywhere.
A light bulb flickers, then it dies,
Guess it's time for bold surprise!

Hands up high, can't find my way,
Stumble, giggle, that's my play!
Who needs a map or fancy guide?
When blindfolded is how we glide!

Falling down the rabbit hole,
Stirring chaos—what a role!
In the dark, we crack a joke,
While mysteries dance, we're just smoke!

So cheer to nights of lost delight,
When wrong turns feel just right.
Embrace the dark, it's all a game,
Where funny quirks are never lame!

Canvas of Uncertainty

With paintbrushes and colors wide,
Let's splash some chaos, let it glide!
A canvas blank, what could it be?
A masterpiece, or chicken spree?

Swirling patterns, just for fun,
Can't quite tell if it's a bun.
Every stroke a laugh, a tease,
Am I creating? Oh, who sees?

Art is fleeting, messy, bright,
Like trying to catch a fly at night.
With every guess, we giggle loud,
Our visions lost inside a cloud.

So let's embrace this artful spree,
Where certainty is a foreign key.
Each blunder forms our quirky mark,
In this bright world, we'll always spark!

The Quiet Thrill of Potential

A balloon floats, what could it be?
Drifting high, who's on the spree?
Could it burst or carry on?
With each balloon there's a new dawn.

Silly cakes await to rise,
With ingredients, oh, what a surprise!
Will it flop or be a treat?
The unknown's funny, can't be beat!

Each moment holds a quirky charm,
Like trying to cook with no alarm.
Dancing, laughing in the unknown,
In every blunder, we've grown!

So let's revel in every chance,
To skip and twirl in this wild dance.
For in the unexpected, we find the thrill,
A playful heart is such a skill!

Embracing the Void

In the spacious unknown, I prance,
Wearing mismatched socks, take a chance.
What's around the corner? Who can tell?
Maybe a party or a wishing well.

With a map upside down in my hand,
I wander through a whimsical land.
A runaway cat leads me astray,
But who needs direction, anyway?

A cloud just whispered a silly plot,
I follow the giggles; I'll take my shot.
With nothing on my calendar stacked,
Surprises bloom where I least expected.

Laughter erupts like a popped balloon,
In not knowing lies the funniest tune.
So let's dance wildly, embrace the tease,
In the void of plans, a life of ease.

The Art of Letting Go

I signed up for yoga, missed the class,
Found an ice cream shop, had a blast.
The instructor's voice still lingers sweet,
But who needs balance when there's a treat?

I tossed my to-do list into the breeze,
It floated away with remarkable ease.
Plans like balloons, they popped and flew,
Now I sip iced coffee with a view.

Each unwritten page feels like a joke,
Just scribble a laugh, let the ink choke.
With every mishap, I find my flow,
Turns out the best art is losing control.

So here's to the chaos, the fun and the glee,
In the wild uncertainty, I'm finally free.
Let go of the map, savor each whim,
And dance to the rhythm of life's lovely hymn.

Unexpected Turns of Fate

I stumbled on a path paved in marshmallows,
And tripped on the gags delivered by shadows.
With fate as my guide and comedy's hand,
Every wrong turn feels just like a band.

A duck in a tie was leading the way,
He quacked out guidelines, hip-hip-hooray!
Life's not a straight line, oh what a bore,
With each goofy twist, I'll always want more.

The road signs are wobbly, but that's just fine,
Each detour I take, I see sunshine (or wine).
A tumble, a roll, and a burst of surprise,
In the circus of life, I'm the clown that flies!

So here's to tomorrow, wild and absurd,
To chasing the whims that never deterred.
With laughter and folly, I'll take each fate,
For who knew confusion could taste so great?

Frolics in the Fog

In the misty bafflement where giggles grow,
I put on my goggles, don't know where to go.
My thoughts bump around like a bouncy ball,
Each idea's a jester, I'm ready to fall.

The fog forms shapes, whimsical and wide,
Like a circus parade that can't decide.
A llama in slippers waves me hello,
While shadows pull pranks, and I laugh in tow.

Chasing my thoughts as they dance out of sight,
I trip over dreams that giggle with fright.
Each silly moment a treasure to share,
With friends in the haze, we float without care.

So here's to the laughter that dwells in the air,
To frolics in fog, we've not a single care.
With foghorns of joy and noses that freeze,
We embrace every giggle that comes with the breeze.

Echoes of Infinite Numina

In a world of absurdity, I roam,
With questions in my pocket, no need for a home.
The universe chuckles, a playful riddle,
As I dance to the beat of a life that's a fiddle.

Uncertainty hums like a bee on a spree,
Buzzing around without a care, oh so free.
A map drawn in crayon, directions unclear,
Still, I wander with laughter, shedding all fear.

Each twist and turn, a chance to delight,
Who knows what's ahead, but it might be all right.
A fortune cookie whispered, 'You'll soon see the sun,'
But the light might just be from a madcap run.

In the echoes of voices from worlds yet unseen,
I cherish the chaos, a life filled with sheen.
So here's to the twists, the turns, and the whim,
The ink's still unfurling, let's dance on a whim!

Transitions in the Mist

Wading through fog with my shoes tied in knots,
The path's like a game of whimsical spots.
I giggle at clues that don't lead anywhere,
With my compass upside down, but who really cares?

The trees seem to whisper sweet secrets and more,
While I trip over roots, finding joy on the floor.
Serendipity dances, elusive like mist,
In the wobbly journey, it's thrill I can't resist.

A sign might say 'lost,' but I'm finding my groove,
With every misstep, I'm starting to move.
Leap after leap, on this wild, balmy trip,
I'm the star of a story, just savor the slip.

Just maybe there's magic in not having plans,
In a world without maps, I'll do my own dance.
With laughter as my guide, I'll float, hop, and twist,
Who needs all the answers when life's such a mist?

Relishing Unwritten Chapters

A book without pages, what a curious sight,
I scribble my thoughts in the dead of the night.
Each line left blank is a wink from the muse,
Where tales are born fresh, with nothing to lose.

I fumble through the plot with my coffee in tow,
Letting the ideas flit, bubble, and flow.
A hero, a villain, I'm both on the page,
What's life without laughter? An empty stage.

The chapters unwritten, they giggle and dance,
Piquant surprises wait, like a well-timed glance.
I relish the chaos, the mess of the pen,
Crafting wild adventures again and again.

So bring on the wonders, the blanks yet to fill,
With comical twists and an insatiable thrill.
In this unwritten tale where absurdity reigns,
The fun is in finding what silly remains!

Unveiling the Beautiful Unknown

Peeling back layers like an onion so sweet,
Each slice is a puzzle, a humorous treat.
I stumble in wonder, who knew it was here?
The beauty of chaos is perfectly clear.

With a map full of arrows pointing nowhere at all,
I tumble through gardens where daisies enthrall.
Unraveling laughter, the petals unfold,
In the garden of 'why not?', surprises grow bold.

The winds tell a story of things left to find,
With giggles and nudges that tickle the mind.
What's better than wandering, lost in good fun?
Each turn of the corner, a laugh just begun.

So here's to tomorrow, with its curious guise,
For how would we know if we never try'd?
The beautiful unknown calls out with delight,
Join me in the mystery, let's dance through the night!

Paths Yet to Unravel

In shoes too big, I waddle on,
Where will I end? A game or con?
With each footfall a giggle spry,
Lost with glee beneath the sky.

A twist, a turn, oh what a sight!
My lunch was last seen, oh what a fright!
Each step an option, wild and bright,
Do I walk straight or take to flight?

The compass spins, it plays a trick,
Left, right, up? Why not all quick?
Adventure waits with a silly grin,
On paths untraveled, let's begin!

So here I dance, with no clear aim,
Life's a game, and I'm to blame!
The wrong turn might just be the best,
In this grand quest, I jest, I fest!

The Beauty of Ambiguity

Shall I wear socks or go on bare?
Mystery hides in my underwear!
It's a puzzle, a riddle dear,
Who knows what's under yonder sphere?

Dinner plans? A feast or fake?
Is that a veggie or a snake?
None can tell, not even me,
Ah, what a joyous calamity!

A songbird chirps; I wish I knew,
If it sings of love or of fondue.
I tap my toes; let's take a chance,
In confusion, I start to dance!

With shades of gray, I paint my day,
Who needs answers? I'd rather play!
Each silly guess a joyful spark,
In the haze, I leave my mark!

Curiosity's Canvas

I dip my brush in mystery's hue,
What's next? A cat or kangaroo?
Swirls of color, a painted tease,
Who knows what art will come with ease?

Shapes that giggle and colors that sing,
What comes from this? A wondrous thing!
Perhaps a tree that wears a hat,
Or a dancing dog, oh imagine that!

Each stroke reveals a wild delight,
Faces that smile, oh what a sight!
With laughter echoing, I create,
A joyful mess, not a clean slate!

A canvas stretches wide and bright,
Every 'oops' turns wrong into right.
With each blunder, my spirit flies,
In curiosity, joy never dies!

A Journey without a Map

A backpack full of snacks and dreams,
Where am I headed? Who knows, it seems!
With laughter, clouds, and airy chats,
The world's my playground, fancy that!

GPS? Nah, I'll wing it bold,
The sun feels warm, the air feels cold.
With a skip and hop, I lose my way,
Oh, isn't that how we play each day?

A signpost points in three directions,
Do I choose chaos or collections?
With giggles loud, I tumble down,
Life's a circus in a silly crown!

Every twist is a jester's jest,
In this wild ride, I feel so blessed.
Without a map, I'll laugh and roam,
For every misstep leads me home!

Dance of the Unfamiliar

In a room full of strangers, I twirl and spin,
My feet have a mind, but they're wearing thin.
I step on a toe, then stumble and sway,
Laughter erupts; I'm the star of the day.

With each awkward dance move, I grin ear to ear,
What's coming next? Oh, nobody's clear.
With a wiggle and jiggle, I jump into space,
Embarrassment? No! Just a delightful race.

Around me, folks chuckle at my fumbling spree,
A conga line forms; it's a whimsical glee.
We twirl and we spin, in this jester's hall,
Who cares about rhythm? We're having a ball!

So here's to the mishaps that break the routine,
In the dance of the clueless, we've found our sheen.
With each misstep, another friend appears,
We've mastered the art of joyful leers.

In the Realm of the Unknown

A map in my pocket, but I've lost my way,
My compass is spinning; is that a café?
I wander through alleys, my sense of direction,
Finding new snacks—oh, what a confection!

I ask for a guide, but they scratch their head,
"Go left at the tulips and right at the shed."
I laugh at the nonsense; it makes perfect sense,
In this world of blunders, I find my pretense.

A street artist winks; I'm drawn to their lines,
Painting my chaos in glorious designs.
With each brushstroke painted, I lose track of time,
Unexpected moments, life's verse and rhyme.

So here's to the paths where the maps all go wrong,
Making sweet melodies, our own little song.
In the realm of the missing, surprises take flight,
In the dance of confusion, we twirl towards the light.

Secrets Hidden in Shadows

Beneath the old bridge, I found something neat,
A sock, a shoe, and a half-eaten treat.
What secrets lie there? What stories untold?
A treasure hunt blooming, vibrant and bold!

As shadows grow longer, I peep 'round the bend,
Will I find hidden treasures or just make a friend?
A curious raccoon gives me quite the glance,
Is he judging my choices or planning to dance?

In corners and alleyways, giggles abound,
With every odd relic, a giggling sound.
What's lost becomes laughter, a light-hearted game,
Finding more joy in the quirky and same.

So here's to the shadows where silliness plays,
In the mix of the odd, we'll spend all our days.
With each foolish venture, life's laughter takes hold,
In the secrets we cherish, we're rich, not just bold.

Serendipity's Embrace

Stumbling through life like a kid on a spree,
Tripping on joy and giggling for free.
Each twist and each turn, a surprise waits ahead,
With cereal dinners and hats filled with dread.

I find rubber ducks where the forks used to be,
Inventing new games, like hopscotch on tea!
The world has no limits when nonsense is near,
Like socks on a turtle, it brings up good cheer.

Oh, the whimsy of life with its twists and its turns,
Unexpected stardust that everyone yearns.
Embracing the odd, like a jester I stand,
Serendipity's magic, ever so grand!

In this dance of the silly, we laugh and we play,
Finding fortune in goofiness—who needs a bouquet?
With hearts full of wonder, we take on each day,
In the tapestry woven with laughter and sway.

Embracing the Unwritten

In a world where plans unfold,
I dance with chaos, brave and bold.
I wear mismatched socks with flair,
Who needs a map? I love the snare.

My coffee's cold, my toast's on fire,
Yet I find joy—my heart's desire.
I trip on dreams while skipping stones,
Adventure calls, my spirit moans.

Pie charts, lists—I toss them all,
Puddles splash; I take the fall.
A mystery awaits around each bend,
Who knows the craziness I'll send?

So let the winds of whims collide,
I'll cheer in chaos, with arms spread wide.
Each moment's a riddle, a puzzle, a game,
Creativity bursts like wild champagne.

Bliss in Uncertainty

A squirrel stole my sandwich today,
I chased it down, but it got away.
Life's twists and turns give me a grin,
What wild tales lie where I've been?

Plans go awry, and that's just fine,
I zig and zag like I'm on a line.
With every wrong step, I take a leap,
Laughing at secrets, both shallow and deep.

The book I'm reading's missing a page,
The plot's a mess; I feel the rage.
But I flip on through, with a chuckle and sigh,
Maybe I'm meant to just wonder why.

So let the universe spin its thread,
With no clue where I'll be led.
I'll sip my tea and just let it be,
Finding bliss in the calamity.

Dancing in the Shadows of Doubt

I waltz on doubts, as if on air,
With shoes too big, I pirouette with flair.
Twirling in circles, I lose my path,
Who needs direction? I'll dance the math.

Mistakes are my partners, we tango with grace,
Each misstep a chance to embrace the space.
Like juggling puzzle pieces that don't quite fit,
I laugh as they scatter—oh, isn't it a hit?

I ask for guidance and get no reply,
Stars seem to giggle as I wonder why.
But in this confusion, I find my fun,
The shadows of doubt dance one by one.

So here's to the clumsy, the hesitant hearts,
Who leap into chaos and embrace all the parts.
For every stumble is a chance to cheer,
Do the funky chicken, and shed all your fear.

Wanderlust for the Unknown

My GPS broke, I'm lost in the park,
The ducks are laughing, all leaping with spark.
Do I seek the road? Or chase after clouds?
In this wild garden, I'm lost in the crowds.

The ice cream truck plays a tune so sweet,
But where's my wallet? Life's a funny feat!
I'll barter with smiles, with goofy grins,
Adventure tomorrow—let the chaos begin!

Maps on my wall are a bit of a joke,
Every line crumbled; I'm veering off smoke.
Each turn's a riddle, a challenge, a quest,
Where will I wander next? That's the fun test!

So here's to the journey, the roads that we take,
With all the wrong turns, and the paths we forsake.
The unknown's a canvas—let colors explode,
For life is a story untold, as we go.

Invisibility of Comfort Zones

In my chair I sit and sway,
Wishing I could sail away.
But what if waves are made of cheese?
Or storms come dressed in polka beads?

Each moment safe, I know so well,
But tedium rings just like a bell.
If I break free, nope, I might find,
A world where socks won't match my mind!

From the shadows, fears take flight,
Once in view, they seldom bite.
What's more frightening than a splash?
A puddle that's now filled with cash!

In the swirl of risk and play,
Magic lives right here today.
Let's skip the maps, avoid the charts,
And dance to tunes that tickle hearts.

Untold Stories Await

In a book with pages bare,
Lie adventures, eyes would stare.
Plot twists wrapped in bubble gum,
Characters that play the drum.

The cycle spins, the pages flip,
Each chapter's a banana slip.
What if dragons prefer to bake?
Or giants love a good flake cake?

Turn the lens and peek inside,
A world with glee we cannot hide.
Tomorrow's plot? A mystery,
With hopeful notes of history!

Every secret dance awaits,
In old cupboards behind the plates.
With a wink and winkled grin,
Let's search the nooks, let's dive in!

Embracing Change's Music

With a wiggle, I await the groove,
A dance that might just disapprove.
Each note a chance to slip and slide,
With rhythms where the weird reside.

Change strums loud on strings so fine,
A melody that's truly mine.
What if I waltz on spaghetti?
Or cha-cha on a bumpy jetty?

Each beat a whim, a playful jest,
What if I trip and feel the best?
A comical fall or a little twirl,
Can spin my world into a whirl!

Join the fun, the laughter rolls,
When toes collide and humor strolls.
So let's leap where musicians throng,
For life's a tune, let's dance along!

The Playfulness of Ambivalence

A puzzle lost, pieces in sight,
Shall I choose dark or leave it light?
With every turn, the game's a laugh,
Do I pick the cat or the giraffe?

In the silliness of 'what might be',
I plant my feet on tangled trees.
A market where all styles collide,
Should I ride the waves or take a slide?

Choosing wrong brings giggles loud,
A tumble here, a shuffle proud.
What's the worst that could derive?
A popcorn crown where we all thrive!

To linger in unsure delight,
Is just the way to ignite the night.
With winks and grins we find our way,
In the maze of choice where we replay!

Mystery's Gentle Lure

In the fridge, a veggie jar,
Is it pickles? Or a star?
I open it with a curious glance,
And a smell leads me to dance.

Where did I leave my left shoe?
Is it hiding or just shy too?
The cat laughs from the windowsill,
As I search with hopeful will.

The mailman drops a mystery pack,
With strange stickers on the back.
Did I win a trip or just a sock?
I tear it open – it's a rock!

Life's a riddle wrapped in cheer,
The answers often disappear.
Each twist and turn makes me grin,
Embracing chaos, let's begin!

When Surprises Bloom

The garden yields unusual sights,
A purple carrot? Oh, what a fright!
I bite into it, expect a crunch,
But it tastes like my old lunch!

The mailbox holds a secret note,
From someone I don't even quote.
A mystery of love or tease?
It's scribbled in crayon – oh, what a breeze!

The dog digs up a shoe from the past,
Was it mine, or did it have a blast?
I wear it as a fashion statement,
Strolling proudly with my entertainment.

Each twist in life brings laughs!
Like spaghetti that breaks into halves.
Surprises bloom where least expected,
And joy is found when we're connected.

Wandering into the Unknown

I wandered into a chocolate shop,
With flavors that make my heart flop.
There's pickle fudge and mustard cream,
Oh, how wild my taste buds dream!

The map I've drawn is upside down,
Leading me straight to the donut town.
Each time I ask for a direction,
I find a cat with a new reflection.

The gas station holds a surprise café,
With coffee brewed from yesterday.
Do I sip it slow or take a gulp?
I choose a dance – the caffeine jolt!

Wandering leads to giggles galore,
Unexpected finds at every door.
Dare to step where few have tread,
Each moment's fun, enough said!

Laughter in the Uncertain

I packed my lunch with zest and cheer,
But what's that? A rubber beer?
Oh, lunchroom jokes go around in style,
As we laugh and ponder for a while.

Directions lead me to a wall,
Was that the turn? Or did I stall?
My GPS just spoke in rhymes,
Each turn I take leads to funny times.

A surprise from my friend in disguise,
Wearing glasses that amplify lies.
We giggle at the joyous schemes,
Building a world out of our dreams.

In each twist, the fun takes flight,
Finding laughter feels so right.
In uncertainty, we'll forever be,
Dancing through life, wild and free!

The Stir of Adventure's Heart

I once embarked on a wild quest,
With half a map and no clear jest.
The compass spun like a child's toy,
Chasing shadows, feeling joy.

I ducked a tree, then tripped on grass,
Met a squirrel with a bit of sass.
It squeaked advice in a nutty tone,
Leaving me puzzled and all alone.

A rogue raccoon stole my snack and ran,
I couldn't help but be his fan.
With every wrong turn, I found delight,
In the chaos, everything felt right.

So here's to journeys with twists and bends,
Where laughter grows and logic ends.
Embrace the mischief, the paths unknown,
Adventure awakens the heart we've sown.

Unmasking the Unexpected

A door swung wide, but no one was there,
I grinned at the chill of the evening air.
A ghost, perhaps, or a cat in disguise,
Hiding away with mischievous eyes.

Glimpses of shadows danced on the wall,
Oh, the fun in the mystery's call.
Finding lost socks, the joys they bring,
Socked puppets that giggle and sing!

A knock on the window—a strange little tap,
A weathered old clown with a fancy hat.
He juggled my worries, made them fall,
Then rolled out a joke to cover it all.

So here's to the laughter when life feels askew,
To each hidden blessing, to spirits anew.
We dance in the whims of the absurd and the bright,
Unmasking the joy in our curious plight.

The Unseen Symphony

Silence fell, and then there came,
A chorus of crickets, playing a game.
I swayed to the rhythm of vines and breeze,
In the hush of the night, a tune to please.

Around me the stars began to hum,
As fireflies joined, a glittery drum.
I tapped my toes on the grass below,
In a concert of nature, a silly show.

A raccoon's duet with a clumsy owl,
Made me laugh 'til I spun like a towel.
The world was a stage, full of delight,
Where humor and chaos partnered all night.

So dance to the music, embrace every sound,
In the unknown journey, fun can be found.
The unseen symphony plays on and on,
Filling the hours with giggles until dawn.

Rejoicing in Surprise

I opened a gift with a curious grin,
Expecting one thing, but oh where to begin?
A rubber duck that quacked 'Hello!'
And a pair of bright socks that danced in a row.

Each twist of the day, a playful surprise,
Like a cake made of broccoli, oh what a prize!
Laughing with friends at the table so wide,
We toasted to chaos, our hearts open wide.

A bubble burst, and a pie flew high,
With whipped cream landing on my nearby pie.
The laughter erupted, we all took a dive,
Rejoicing in moments that keep us alive.

So here's to the surprises that tickle and tease,
That fill up our homes and hearts with such ease.
In the quilt of our stories, woven so bright,
We find joy in the randomness, day and night.

Whims of Fortuity

A squirrel stole my sandwich, oh dear,
I laughed as he danced with a sneer.
What should I expect from today?
Maybe a raccoon will lead the way!

Who knows where the lost socks will go?
To a party with gnomes? What a show!
Each twist brings a tingle of cheer,
Embracing the chaos, I shed my fear.

A bump on my head from a low-flying kite,
Was it chance or fate, who's to indict?
In the realm of the silly and absurd,
Each moment whispers, "You've never heard!"

So let's hop on this train to who-knows-where,
With dancing llamas and fresh mountain air.
The world spins on whims, and I'm happy to play,
With serendipity guiding my day-to-day.

Embracing the Beautiful What-ifs

What if ducks wore hats, oh what a delight,
In a quacky parade, they'd snag every sight.
Imagine the giggles, the splashes so bright,
As they waddle along in the evening light.

I ponder the thoughts drifting lazily round,
Like clouds in the sky, or a lost golden hound.
What if my fridge could chat and tell jokes?
Would it laugh at my midnight munching, oh folks!

There's magic in pondering paths not yet tried,
Each turn whispers secrets that dare to confide.
What if today's fate brought a pie to my door?
"Surprise!" cries the universe, "Here's even more!"

So etched in these musings are moments to spare,
A tapestry woven with whimsical flair.
In life's jumbled puzzle, let laughter unfurl,
As we dive into the "what-ifs" of this world.

Flights of Fancy in Twilight

What if owls wore glasses to read at night?
In debates with the moon, they'd engage in flight.
Sipping tea with the stars, so oddly polite,
These creatures of whimsy, what a curious sight!

The fireflies whisper sweet nothings in dark,
While bears try to dance, oh what a lark!
What's brewing in dreams, a wild frolic spree?
Perhaps we'll wake up and find glee!

A dandelion turning to fluff on the breeze,
Can hold all my hopes, my giggles, my tease.
What if a rainbow could jump through the air?
With unicorns riding, we'd breathe in the fair!

So onward we wander in twilight's embrace,
With bubbles of laughter and joy in each space.
In tales woven bright, let our spirits take flight,
As we dance through the shadows, exchanging delight.

Riddles of Radiance

Pineapple on pizza? A curious choice,
As I ponder the flavors, I giggle, rejoice.
What if spaghetti grew tall in the sun?
In a world full of wonders, we've only begun!

Let's turn our frowns into rainclouds of cheer,
What riddles can sparkle and laugh in our sphere?
Perhaps shoes made of marshmallows would do,
To bounce off the pavement, like dreams coming true!

I trip on a question, it laughs as I stumble,
With each twist of the tale, I burst forth with a grumble.
What if the toothpaste could sing from the tube?
In concerts of colors, we'd join the fun groove!

So here's to the riddles that twirl and they spin,
With giggles and sparkles, let the nonsense begin.
In this wacky ballet of life on display,
We embrace every whim, come what may!

Sweetness in the Unwritten

There's a charm in unanswered quests,
Maps that lead nowhere are the best.
The treasure's a laugh, not gold in a chest,
As we juggle our queries like a bold jest.

With questions afloat like balloons in the air,
We dance round the logic, without a care.
What's the recipe for life, just a flair?
Mix in a giggle, a pinch of a dare.

Mistakes? They're just plots, twists in our fate,
With every 'oops' comes a twist oh so great.
Let's toast to the chaos, it tastes like a plate,
Of confusion served warm—dare we relate?

In this book full of blank, we sip from our cups,
Savoring moments as time gently interrupts.
So here's to the tales that fortune disrupts,
We write our own stories with happy hiccups.

Echoes of What If

What if the squirrel ran the race of the day?
Would acorns be trophies or just child's play?
If clouds were made of candy, come what may,
We'd still end up lost in the cosmic ballet.

Tick-tock of the clock, but where does it go?
Bouncing like bunnies in fanciful flow.
Oh, the giggles we'd find in the pot of woe,
As 'what if' spins tales in a whimsical show.

Each guess is an adventure, each whim is a song,
In the realm of the unknown, we can't go wrong.
So let's skip down the lanes where the oddballs belong,
With 'maybe' as our anthem, we'll merrily throng.

We stumble through life like a clown on a spree,
Finding joy in the quirks that simply won't flee.
Each 'what if' a ticket, come join in with glee,
In this circus of thoughts, we're forever so free.

The Adventure of Not Knowing

Let's pack our bags with the unknowns we crave,
We'll surf on the waves of the whims that we pave.
Maps are for losers, the bold will be brave,
Drink the nectar of chaos, our minds will misbehave.

The compass is broken, but who really cares?
We follow the laughter, it's hiding downstairs.
With questions like umbrellas, we toss them in flares,
And dance in the puddles without any snares.

Should we pet a llama or teach frogs to sing?
Every choice is a delight, let your heart take wing.
In this carnival mindset, we'll laugh like a king,
Each leap into madness is our favorite fling.

So grab the confetti, let's sprinkle some cheer,
Each moment mysterious becomes crystal clear.
With a wink and a grin, let's throw out all fear,
In this adventure of life, we hold treasures near.

Ambling in Enigma

Strolling down paths with no signs in sight,
We giggle at shadows that playfully bite.
With riddles like candy, they're hard but so bright,
In the game of confusion, we're winning the fight.

Puddles of ponder, we hop and we splash,
Questions like fireflies that flash in a dash.
Each twist in the story, a delightful mash,
Maybe we'll stumble but never we'll crash.

In the maze of the silly, we swirl and we spin,
With chuckles like music, we revel within.
Every turn is a canvas, let the fun begin,
In this leaves-fall dance, we just can't help but grin.

Embrace the unknown, wear a balloon hat,
Whistle through whims, as we follow the cat.
Life's a great party, all fluffy and fat,
In the mystery's realm, let's just chat and pat!

www.ingramcontent.com/pod-product-compliance
Lightning Source LLC
Chambersburg PA
CBHW051633160426
43209CB00004B/632